Sounds True, Inc., Boulder CO 80306
© 2005, 2010 Sharon Salzberg

SOUNDS TRUE is a trademark of Sounds True, Inc.

Published 2010
Cover and book design by Rachael Murray

Printed in Canada

ISBN: 978-1-59179-920-7

Library of Congress Control Number: 2005927089

10 9 8 7 6 5 4

Sharon Salzberg

The Force of Kindness

Change Your Life with Love & Compassion

SOUNDS TRUE
Boulder, CO 80306

contents

Introduction

I have been engaged by kindness nearly my whole life, fascinated by it at times, repulsed by it at others. Particularly when I was young and others extended kindness to me, I felt humiliated by the apparent evidence of my pain. I hated that anyone could see that I was hurt. And yet, now I see that those early gifts of kindness planted the seeds of a nascent self-love within me. Those seeds were really what allowed me, more than anything else, to survive the often painful circumstances of my childhood. As I got older, I was less resistant to acts of kindness, more moved by them, more able to acknowledge how important they had been and still were to me.

Since then, the pursuit of kindness has magnetized much of my spiritual journey—that is, once I got over my disdain of it as an "also-ran" quality, the kind of characteristic you cultivate if tougher, finer things like wisdom elude you. As I continue my meditation practice every day and try to live out my deepest values every day, kindness has only grown in importance as a crucial element of those efforts.

It is not a cushy, undemanding path. It is easy to overlook the power of kindness or misunderstand it. The embodiment of kindness is often made difficult by our long-ingrained patterns of fear and jealousy. Those around us may devalue our dedication to kindness. We may devalue it ourselves. There are many challenges, many subtleties, many intricacies. But if we can commit to the open-hearted exploration of kindness, it will reveal itself as a force that can change our lives.

—Sharon Salzberg

"Kindness"

Before you know what kindness really is
you must lose things,
feel the future dissolve in a moment
like salt in a weakened broth.
What you held in your hand,
what you counted and carefully saved,
all this must go so you know
how desolate the landscape can be
between the regions of kindness.
How you ride and ride
thinking the bus will never stop,
the passengers eating maize and chicken
will stare out of the window forever.

Before you learn the tender gravity of kindness,
you must travel where the Indian in a white poncho
lies dead by the side of the road.
You must see how this could be you,
how he too was someone
who journeyed through the night with plans
and the simple breath that kept him alive.

Introduction

Before you know kindness as the deepest thing inside,
you must know sorrow as the other deepest thing.
You must wake up with sorrow.
You must speak to it till your voice
Catches the thread of all sorrows
And you see the size of the cloth.

Then it is only kindness that makes sense anymore,
only kindness that ties your shoes
and sends you out into the day to mail letters and purchase bread,
only kindness that raises its head from the crowd of the world to say
It is I you have been looking for,
and then goes with you everywhere
like a shadow or a friend.

—Naomi Shihab Nye

one

Compassion in Action

K indness is compassion in action. It is a way of taking the vital human emotions of empathy or sympathy and channeling those emotions into a real-life confrontation with ruthlessness, abandonment, thoughtlessness, loneliness—all the myriad ways, every single day, we find ourselves suffering or witnessing suffering in others.

Yet growing up I had the impression that a kind heart ranked awfully low in cultural desirability, well after a sound head, a sharp wit, invulnerability, power over others, a fine sense of irony, and countless other qualities. The hero I saw displayed in the movies was fiercely resolute; the sidekick, trailing after the hero, picking up the pieces, might have been

kind. The overwhelmingly popular girl on TV was striking, imposing, amusing; the second banana was usually kind and a lot less magnetic or interesting.

Today as well, when we think of adventure, going out on a limb, being bold, or being on the edge, it is rarely in the direction of caring, of compassion. Usually we externalize our sense of adventure and think of climbing mountains or jumping out of airplanes. Our idea of taking a risk is to be more ambitious, maybe more competitive. To be bold translates as being more hard-bitten and not noticing the consequence of our actions on others. To be brave has no gentleness or sensitivity associated with it.

On the face of it, kindness can seem wimpy, a cop-out, an excuse to do just a little bit to try to make a difference when so very much needs to be done. We might see kindness as the rationale for feeling good after speaking nicely to a homeless person we meet on the street, without having to consider basic injustice and what steps have to be taken to help that person and others like him or her to not suffer anymore. We might delegate kindness to the category of a quaint, old-fashioned virtue—not very effective, and certainly not very powerful. We might disdain kindness as a way of promoting separation and a hierarchy of distinctions: "I, who am superior and untouched by your problem, will help you, who are inferior and in a bad way." We might dismiss kindness as the last, frail stand of righteousness—the lesser state we turn to in some

dismay when wisdom, clarity, incisiveness, and intense love all have seemed to fail us and we haven't been able to make any substantial difference in someone's life.

A commitment to kindness can be the thread that twines throughout our various successes, disappointments, delights, and traumas, making our lives seamless, giving us ballast in a world of change, a reservoir of heartfulness to infuse our choices, our relationships, and our reactions.

Many of us long for an underlying sense of meaning, something we can still believe in no matter what happens to us, a navigational force to pull all the disparate pieces of our lives together into some kind of whole. Perhaps we find ourselves feeling helpless when even a little too much of the unexpected occurs. Or we feel defenseless when we find we don't have control over a situation and can't fathom what might happen next, unsure of where to turn when we aren't having the positive effect we want with a troubled family member or a friend. In any of these circumstances, and in so many more, we shut down. Then we go through the motions of our day, day after day, without much dynamism or spirit.

Many of us experience ourselves as fragmented, perhaps as confident and expressive when we are with our families but a

completely different person when we are at work, frequently hesitant and unsure. Perhaps we take risks when we are with others but are timid when alone, or we are cozily comfortable when alone yet are painfully shy and withdrawn when with others. Or maybe we drift along with the tides of circumstance, going up and down, not knowing what we might really care about more than anything else, but thinking there must be *something*.

To explore kindness as that thread of meaning requires finding out if we can be strong and still be kind, be smart and still be kind, whether we can be profoundly kind to ourselves and at the same time strongly dedicated to kindness for those around us. We have to find the power in kindness, the confidence in kindness, the release in kindness—the type of kindness that transcends belief systems, allegiances, ideologies, cliques, and tribes. This is the trait that can transform our lives.

Kindness is the fuel that helps us truly "walk our talk" of love, a quality so easy to speak about or extol but often so hard to make real. It helps us to genuinely care for one another and for ourselves as well. Kindness is the foundation of unself-conscious generosity, natural inclusivity, and an unfeigned integrity. When we are devoted to the development of kindness, it becomes our ready response, so that reacting from compassion, from caring, is not a question of giving ourselves a lecture: "I don't really feel like it, but I'd better be helpful, or what would people think?" When we are devoted to the

development of kindness, we are no longer forcing ourselves into a mold we think we have to occupy; rather, it becomes a movement of the heart so deep and subtle that it is like a movement of the sea close to the ocean floor, all but hidden yet affecting absolutely everything that happens above. That's the force of kindness.

The quality of kindness gives us the ability to take abstract ideals like compassion, or "love thy neighbor," and make them authentic and palpable and vibrant each and every day, going to work or going to school or going home, or getting through a situation we would never in a million years have chosen. When we really examine kindness we find it is a deep and abiding understanding of how connected we all are. We see that kindness inspires a sense of ethics independent of any religious adherence, which can guide our families, communities, and the world we live in toward realizing greater safety and peace. I think this spirit underlies one of His Holiness the Dalai Lama's most famous quotations: "My true religion is kindness."

In 1997, while attending a conference in San Francisco called "Peacemaking: The Power of Nonviolence," I walked by the writer Alice Walker, who was having an informal conversation with a group of people. I overheard her say, "As I get older, I realize that the thing I value the most is good-heartedness." Intrigued, I reflected for some time on that statement. I thought of how we struggle and strive in life, of our craving for acquisitions and attainments and possessions and praise and glory. Then I

thought of what in fact uplifts us when we are feeling down no matter how much we own, of what gives us a boost when it is so easy to feel weak or inferior because we are in mental or physical pain. I thought of what unites us when we could, instead, feel isolated or hurt because of some difference that we think sets us intractably apart, or one that others deliberately use to marginalize or diminish us. And I too found myself again and again coming back to good-heartedness, to the giving and receiving of kindness.

From birth, and in fact well before, we are dependent on someone's kindness. An infant who is being severely deprived of basic emotional sustenance, even though physically well cared for, can fail to thrive and can eventually die. We need affection, nurturing, and attention, not just to embellish our life or to have a somewhat better day, but for our actual survival. And in the absence of receiving this kindness, something in us does die, at least for a while, unless and until it can be restored through love.

When the adult daughter of a friend of mine had a child after several years of hoping and trying and had tended to the baby at home for about two weeks, she turned to her mother and said, "You did *this* for me!" The intensity of kindness

needed to consistently put a child's needs ahead of one's own desires can probably be weighed by how many people feel terribly scarred by their childhoods … yet day in and day out, parents and caretakers wake up in the middle of the night or kiss boo-boos or play with Legos endlessly or read *Goodnight Moon* for the millionth time. A friend of mine, a very successful lawyer and an admired public servant, touched upon the awesome quality of this relationship when she, without a moment's hesitation, referred to raising her son as "the most important thing I will ever do in life."

Kindness points to the core of what it means to be alive, which is to be connected. When someone looks at us with the concern of kindness, the sense of connection expressed in her or his eyes reflects our own value. When someone treats us with the benevolence of kindness, the sense of connection informing their actions confirms our own right to be happy. And when someone feels connected enough to reach out to us in kindness, we hear the unspoken message of their efforts—that we are worth the bother.

One of the ways kindness affects us is through the development of "self-efficacy," a contemporary psychological concept that describes a certain kind of faith in ourselves, in our ability to meet difficulties. This quality influences our willingness to take risks, to face new challenges. Albert Bandura, a Stanford psychologist who has done much of the research on self-efficacy, says this: "People's beliefs about their abilities

have a profound effect on those abilities. Ability is not a fixed property . . . there is huge variability in it; people who have a sense of self-efficacy bounce back from failures; they approach things in terms of how to handle them rather than worrying about what can go wrong."

This is the difference between pain and hopelessness, between distress and bitterness, between suffering and despair—sorrows or difficulties arise, yet we have some sense of confidence that we can find a way to work through them. What I found compelling about Dr. Bandura's quotation is the understanding that a person's belief about his or her own abilities has such a strong impact. If ability is not a preordained, limited commodity, then our potential to grow, to understand, to love, to connect is significantly nourished by what we believe about ourselves. This is one of the great fruits of the kindness we receive from others—it supports our sense of being someone deserving of love, someone who can in turn accomplish something, who can vanquish difficulties, who can make it through the travails of life, who can be a good person.

Those who do not receive enough care and kindness at home as a child are sometimes lucky enough to find it at school, later on with a friend or a beloved, or with a spiritual teacher.

This is the source of the pop-culture phrase "It's never too late to have a happy childhood" and of clear insights, such as my own, that one's spiritual teachers can basically re-parent their students. My teachers taught me, through their kindness, that I was capable of wisdom and love, perhaps more so than I had ever imagined.

In fact, this is the role of a spiritual teacher almost by definition: to serve as our mirror, reflecting back to us again and again, "Achievement is possible for somebody just like you." There is a classical phrase in Tibetan Buddhism where someone will refer to his or her meditation teacher as having been "very kind to me." I have heard several generations of Tibetans refer to their teachers first and foremost in terms of their kindness, before mentioning their scholarship or their meditative attainment, before commending their level of prowess at discourse or debate.

It is someone's kindness that essentially affirms us, that conveys a sense of the wholeness they glimpse in us, a wholeness that we ourselves might barely realize. Yet that kindness is not necessarily at all passive or meek. The manifestation of kindness is not just in being nice and sweet—it has great forcefulness. The certainty of someone's conviction that we can be happy, manifested through their caring, animates a potential within us that might otherwise just have lain dormant because we simply did not believe in it. If there is a fire within these spiritual teachers to be truthful, to wake up, to

not waste one's life, as they reach out to us in compassion and bring us close, it can light a similar fire within us as well. And if there is love and peace and humor within them, as they dissolve the apparent differences between us through their acts of kindness, their selflessness can return us to the best in ourselves and help us go on.

In 2004, I was fortunate to be able to join about 7,200 people from fifty-five countries in Toronto, where the Dalai Lama conferred the Kalachakra Initiation. It was an extraordinary eleven-day event that included meditation periods, teachings, and ritual practices. Manifesting his ecumenical spirit, the Dalai Lama liked to begin the afternoon sessions with chanting from the various Buddhist schools represented in the audience. He asked for a rotation that reflected the historical movement of Buddhism around the world and through the centuries, beginning with the Theravada school in India and Southeast Asia, moving through the Mahayana schools of China, Korea, and Japan.

On the initial afternoon, the first to chant were a Canadian monk and an American nun, both ordained in the Theravada tradition, and all went well. On the second afternoon, however, the monk wasn't there, thus the nun was forced to chant all alone in front of the Dalai Lama and all those thousands of people. Many of us would consider it amongst our very worst nightmares to have to sing publicly, facing massive crowds of strangers—let alone to sing right in front of the Dalai Lama.

Because most of my early meditation training was in the Theravada tradition, I more or less knew the particular chants the nun was attempting. I found her so brave as her little wobbly voice plowed through, sometimes reciting just once the refrains meant to be done three times, sometimes confusing the order. I felt so deeply for her. Then after a seeming eternity it was over, and a group representing another country took up the next round.

At the end of the whole rotation, the Dalai Lama paused to thank everyone who had taken part in the chanting and then went on to especially thank the nun who had chanted all by herself, commenting on how very difficult a thing like that is to do. His face beaming with humor and kindness, he went on to describe a time when he had gone to Japan and ended up being asked to chant the Heart Sutra, a fundamental Buddhist text, all alone. He complied, but now looking back, the Dalai Lama said that he feared he had made so many errors, he basically had made up a whole new Heart Sutra! Having told this story about his own imperfection, he burst out laughing.

Later in the afternoon, the American nun, whom I knew slightly, came up to me in the audience. She was radiant, transported from feeling embarrassed by her mistakes to a place of tremendous joy because of the Dalai Lama's comments. The openness of his compassion had freed within her a sense of closeness to everyone rather than the awful aloneness that coils round and round us when we have been anything less than perfect.

Kindness is a practice of inclining the mind, of intention. Rather than laying a veneer of idealism on top of reality, we want to see quite nakedly all the different things that we feel and want for what they are. Perhaps it is anger or fear or repulsion rather than the kindness we would so much more strongly prefer. The mistake that most of us make at one time or another with a practice like compassion or kindness is to try to deny what is actually going on: "I mustn't feel resentment; I must only feel love. Because, after all, that is my dedication—to be kind."

It is a very delicate balance to bring together pure awareness, which is completely honest in seeing what is happening, with an unwavering confidence that reminds us we are genuinely capable of love and compassion. We manage to do so to some extent by practicing love and kindness toward ourselves and by seeing the negative feelings that arise as not our fault. We must learn to view the fact that we have negative feelings not as an irreversible personal defect or as some kind of portentous setback on our path to liberation, but simply as the result of conditioned habits of mind. We can hold both a vision of our heart's objective and a compassionate acknowledgment of whatever truth is manifesting in the present moment.

Even the Dalai Lama says about himself, "I don't know why people like me so much." And then he says, "It must be because

I try to be compassionate, to have bodhicitta, that aspiration of compassion." *Bodhicitta* is the bedrock of Tibetan Buddhism, a wish for the happiness, welfare, and freedom from suffering for all beings everywhere, along with the commitment to work toward that end. Notably, even the Dalai Lama doesn't claim complete success; he claims a dedication to really trying.

Ways of Increasing the Force of Kindness in Your Life
- Reflect on someone in your life who has reached out to you in kindness. How do you regard him or her?
- Notice how the mood of someone in a chance encounter—such as the checkout person in the supermarket or a bank teller—affects you.
- Think about your degree of confidence in yourself. What factors have helped enhance it or decrease it?
- Reflect on why kindness might be considered a force instead of a weakness.
- Make the effort to thank someone each day. Notice what is created between you and the other person in that way.
- Reflect on who you admire in life, and why.

two

Kindness toward Ourselves

We can easily go from morning until night caught in self-preoccupation, nearly constantly thinking, "How do they view me? Does he like me more than he likes her? Is she impressed with me? Am I winning? Am I a complete loser? Am I revealing too much? Could I be perceived as too hidden?"

I saw this tendency in myself when, in September of 2004, I was on tour for my book *Faith: Trusting Your Own Deepest Experience*. As happens on a book tour, I moved quickly from city to city. On September 11 I was going to fly into Washington D.C., give a talk, and then attend a memorial service at the National Cathedral led by the Dalai Lama.

Earlier that week, in Houston, I picked up my cell phone messages. A friend who arranged the Dalai Lama's visit to the Cathedral had called, saying that a Buddhist monk, scheduled to open the program with a reading, had suddenly been called away. She wondered if I might substitute. Remarkably, my first thought upon hearing about this enormous honor was to think, "I don't have the right shoes."

My mind started racing: "Tomorrow I'll be in Minneapolis, but I'll be busy all afternoon. The next day, September 10, I'll be in Chicago. I can get a cab downtown and buy some shoes." Quandary resolved, I returned her call and said, "I'd love to do it."

That night she called back, saying the monk had found a replacement himself, another monk, and I wasn't needed. Released from having to shop, I continued the tour, and on the morning of September 11 flew from Chicago to D.C.

That afternoon I entered the awe-inspiring cathedral, the sixth largest cathedral in the world, still filled with the distinctive sorrow brought up by flying on that particular day. I was also tremendously eager to see the Dalai Lama, whom I hadn't seen in more than a year. Saddened, awed, joyful, excited, I sat there. But as the ceremony started, I found my attention telescope to the substitute monk's feet, gazing intently at his shoes. The majesty of the cathedral disappeared, the somberness of the day receded, even the Dalai Lama went into the background as I looked at the monk's shoes and thought about what mine might have been.

It's a big, rich, intricately textured world, and we often miss most of it because our gaze has narrowed to ourselves, to some facet of how we are appearing to the world, or what others might be thinking about us, now or later. Some examples are ridiculous, as in the previous story, but as the experience of self-preoccupation deepens so does our loneliness, our pain at being cut off, our anxiety, and ultimately our sense of desolation.

This kind of compulsive concern with "I, me, and mine" isn't the same as loving ourselves, just as shallow martyrdom where we only think of others and never care about ourselves isn't really generosity, because both are coming from the wrong intention. Loving ourselves points us to capacities of resilience, compassion, and understanding within that are simply part of being alive.

These capacities are said in Buddhist teaching to be shared by everyone, though they may be quite untapped, hidden, or obscured. If we are in touch with them inside us, we also feel much closer to others because that same potential—seen or unseen, actualized or wasted—exists within all beings, and we recognize that. Obsessive self-interest, in contrast, anchors our sense of who we are squarely in our clinging and our fears. We secretly feel we do not have enough; we are not enough; we are deficient; we are defective. We become preoccupied with trying to acquire enough objects—totems against change and loss—because we are really so afraid. We seek to dominate the world around us and control those we encounter by demanding

affirmation so that we will not be overcome by our own doubts. We go into a room and try to draw the energy there into us, but it never fills us. This isn't love for ourselves; it is more like sorrow strategically and carefully contained.

Loving ourselves opens us to truly knowing ourselves as part of a matrix of existence, inextricably connected to the boundlessness of life. When we keep opening past any version of who we are that is crafted by others, when we see that we are far bigger than the person who is delineated by family or cultural expectations, we realize that we are capable of so much more than we usually dare to imagine. In this spirit the poet Walt Whitman wrote, "I am larger and better than I thought, I did not think I held so much goodness."

Yet we might find it far easier to fixate on our bad choices, on the mistakes we've made, on the time we stayed silent because we were too timid to speak out, on the afternoon we blurted out a statement without any sensitivity to the consequences, on the awkward incident where now, looking back ashamed, we yearn more than anything in the world to be able to somehow erase it all because we were just so wrong.

An interesting distinction can be made in Buddhist psychology between the state of remorse and the state of guilt.

Remorse is considered a skillful state of mind. We recognize that we have said something or done something that has created harm in some way, and we experience the pain of that. But because we essentially forgive ourselves we can let go, and thus we have the energy, the inspiration, not to go on repeating the same mistakes. We need the courage to learn from our past and not live in it.

Guilt, on the other hand, is considered unskillful, because of the component of lacerating self-hatred in it. We go over and over the harmful thing we have done, continually blaming ourselves, stuck there until we are drained. The result is that we are left with no energy to actually transform our actions. We all know those days riddled with guilt—the open acknowledgment of the harm we've caused subsumed by a wave of disbelief that we can ever do better. The honest realization of the disharmony we have created takes second stage to a conviction in our supposed enduring and everlasting immorality.

So while we heal in part by realizing where we've acted wrongly and by feeling genuine remorse, we heal much more completely by remembering that the damaging actions that we recollect are only a part of who we are and of who we might yet become.

Toward that end, a traditional Buddhist contemplation practice is to think of the good within us: the good we have done, the potential for good we can activate. We reflect on the skillful or wholesome actions we've done, on the times we've

had difficult choices to make in areas of morality, and on the times we have tried to be truthful or loving. We reflect on the times we have cared enough to reach out beyond our timidity, on the ways in which we've tried to help someone instead of just carelessly letting the chance go by.

The Buddha taught this practice of reflection, obviously not for the cultivation of conceit or arrogance or to increase our neurotic self-preoccupation. He offered this teaching because even if these times of goodness have been fleeting accomplishments, recalling them can fill us with buoyancy and lightness of heart. They remind us of all we are capable of being and help us determine how to live out our aspirations more fully, instead of merely thinking about our deepest values as distant abstractions that we can never achieve. This kind of contemplation becomes the impetus for leading a better life, because we truly believe we can. This becomes the compassionate context in which we can honestly and directly look at the times we have not been so skillful, and go beyond them.

When we find ourselves dismissing our good actions or rejecting any real chance of change, dwelling in a sense of dissatisfaction, convinced that we don't have enough and we are not enough, we feel impoverished and alone. If we are practicing this reflection acknowledging the good within us, a commitment to change isn't about despair or depression over who we are right now; it's not dispirited. We aren't coming from a place of hopelessness, as though not really believing

there could be any more to us than our recklessness and our faults. We know there is a bigger picture of who we are, and we trust in it. Then we become galvanized to actualize it.

This outlook lies directly upon the path the Buddha taught, commonly known as the middle way. It is called the middle way because it avoids different sets of extremes that we are commonly pulled by and sometimes pulled apart by. The middle way first avoids the extreme of overindulgence in the senses, where we rely on fleeting experiences of pleasure to provide our deepest sense of happiness.

The world of indulgence is intoxicating but hollow, and it surrounds us in a fog that keeps us from looking for anything beyond what we can acquire or consume or help ourselves to right now. Meanwhile, when we are intoxicated with the senses, the suffering of others threatens the feel-good complacency that accompanies our indulgence. Then we tend to disregard the suffering around us, along with trying to cover up whatever internal suffering we may have. And so we end up cut off from whole landscapes of our inner world and are more isolated from the totality of life.

The other extreme avoided by the middle path is that of self-mortification, where we apply various torments of the

body, severe asceticism, or drastic renunciation. It was quite common in the Buddha's time for people in India to feel that by tormenting the body in some way they could liberate the spirit so it would soar free, beyond the strictures pressing in on it from the conditions of this life.

Perhaps some of the practices seen so often in these times such as eating disorders, the habitual cutting or burning of the body, and other compulsive self-injurious behaviors, are something of a modern-day equivalent. Here also we abuse this body, perhaps in hope of finding an ineffable, elusive freedom from pain.

Even more predominant these days is the tendency to get into some kind of punishing relationship with our minds, in which we practice intense criticism and self-deprecation, feeling that somehow these will prove to be a viable path to an improved life. We are disgusted by our fears, frightened by our desires, ashamed of our anxiety, and we struggle tremendously with our tumultuous, cascading emotions. When we take a wrong step, we feel disgraced. When we fail to impress, we ascribe that to something unlikable and irredeemable within us. When we experience loss or pain or sorrow, we feel personally humiliated. We anguish over our disappointed expectations, and we retaliate against our own minds by hating our lack of control, which transforms into hating ourselves.

Our movement away from these extremes onto the middle way is fueled by learning more kindness toward ourselves.

We see the tension, the stress, and the unhappiness of each extreme and come to a completely different place that doesn't fall into either category. A complete revisioning of ourselves, of what we are capable of, and of where happiness is to be found unfolds the middle way before us, step by step.

It is because we learn to love and care for ourselves that we don't want a life glutted by possessions, stimulation, objects, and experiences that we amass mindlessly, compelled because we don't know what else to do when we wake up in the morning in order to feel alive. It is because we learn to love and care for ourselves that we move away from deifying any voice within that mocks us, humiliates us, and mercilessly puts us down. It is because we learn to love and care for ourselves that we apply intelligence and effort to having a better, happier life, and we are willing to go beyond what is merely familiar or convenient.

Part of that revisioning process is to see our own anger and fear and jealousy—and all such states—as suffering rather than as being bad or wrong or contemptible. Then we can have some compassion when we face these states within, and by extension, when we see them at play in others. We can learn not to get engulfed by these states, so that they do not define our world, do not guide us into actions we will later regret. Then as we continue to develop greater love and care toward ourselves, we can go beyond the reflexive, inhibiting habit of self-absorption to find a way to happiness that actually works.

A cornerstone of the Buddha's way to developing genuine happiness is metta meditation. *Metta* is a word in Pali, the language of the original Buddhist texts, that means loving-kindness or friendship. Metta involves silently repeating phrases that offer good qualities to oneself and to others. (The full practice is described on page 27.) It is part of the living tradition of meditation practices that cultivate spaciousness of mind and openness of heart. Classically, metta is taught along with meditations that develop compassion, sympathetic joy (the ability to rejoice in the happiness of others), and equanimity. Together these four are known as the Brahma Viharas. *Brahma* means supreme, or best. *Vihara* means abiding or home. So the Brahma Viharas represent our heart's most supreme abiding, our best home. Metta is the foundation practice of the Brahma Viharas.

Underlying our usual patterns of self-preoccupation, stinging self-judgment, and fear is the universal, innate potential for love and awareness. Metta meditations are based on gently practicing the reflections and actions that point us back to that nascent place within, to feel more comfortable abiding there, to be able to cultivate the love found there and help it flourish.

The flavor of kindness permeates this entire meditation, from the continual refinement of our motives for doing the

practice, to the skillful means we employ when we need to per-
severe in the face of difficulty, to the patience needed to forgive
ourselves and begin again after being distracted and forgetful.

Metta is considered a concentration practice, which means
that we have an object we have chosen to focus on, and we
continually shepherd our minds back to it whenever we notice
our attention has wandered.

Imagine just for a moment the amount of energy you
expend in being lost in brooding over the future, in obsessive
planning, in ruminating about the past, in comparing yourself
to others, in judging yourself, in worrying about what might
happen next. That is a huge amount of energy. Now imagine
all of that energy gathered in, returned to you, available to you.

The return of that enormous amount of energy, normally
dissipated and lost to us, is why concentration practice is so
healing and empowering. We experience wholeness, the unifi-
cation of our being, as we gather this energy back in. What is
striking is the fact that this is our own energy—we don't have
to contemplate the daunting task of somehow finding it or fab-
ricating it. It is our own, but we ordinarily waste quite a bit of it.

Concentration may be difficult to develop at first. We may
be beset by sleepiness as we are getting more relaxed, with the
line between relaxation and sluggishness very blurred. We may
find a remarkable degree of restlessness and agitation within, as
thinking and planning and worrying bubble up. There might
be wild swings of desire and attachment that seem to come

out of nowhere. Sudden anger or impatience might fill us. We might have onslaughts of doubt as we wonder why in the world we are sitting there, attempting to concentrate on such phrases. All of these experiences are natural, and if we relate to them with gentle awareness and compassion for ourselves, they may come up, but they won't dominate. We need just be patient and persistent.

It is important to note, too, that we don't mistake the phrases of metta for some sort of magical thinking. If we say the phrase, "May I be healthy," over and over again, for example, it does not follow that we will never be sick. Rather, we are using the phrase as a way of surrounding ourselves with benefi- cence and good will instead of disparaging ourselves or carping at ourselves.

People often find some difficulty in caring for themselves, in receiving love, in believing they deserve to be happy. Developing care toward ourselves with the power of concentration is the first objective, the foundation for later being able to include others and finally all of life in the sphere of kindness.

Ways of Developing Kindness toward Ourselves
- Spend some time consciously reflecting on the good you've done or a good quality you have.
- Remember a time you made a mistake. What qualities help you learn to act differently? What qualities stifle the creative urge to change?

- If you see anger, fear, or similar states arising in your mind, and you find yourself reacting to them as "bad" or "wrong," purposefully translate that response to "painful" or "suffering." See what changes.
- Reflect on what the middle way might look like for you in a particular endeavor, relationship, or challenge.
- Devote some time each day to self-care. Can you spend fifteen or twenty minutes doing something to be kind to yourself?
- Develop and practice a lovingkindness meditation for yourself (see below).

MEDITATION
Lovingkindness toward Ourselves

Metta meditation practice begins with the suggestion of the Buddha: "Sit comfortably." We achieve this emotionally or psychologically by not striving to have something special happen. Most simply, we assume a comfortable sitting position so we can more easily relax and let go of any sense of struggle.

You can start by taking delight in your own goodness (as described earlier), calling to mind things you have done out of good-heartedness, and rejoicing in those memories to celebrate the potential for goodness we all share.

We silently repeat phrases that reflect what we wish most deeply for ourselves in an enduring way. Traditional phrases are:

- May I live in safety.
- May I have mental happiness (peace, joy).

- May I have physical happiness (health, freedom from pain).
- May I live with ease. (May the elements of daily life—work, family—go easily, not be a struggle.)

You can use these phrases or others that are more personally meaningful to you.

Whenever your attention wanders away from the phrases, gently return to them. This process of shepherding your attention back whenever it has wandered is the act of concentration.

When you practice metta, relax and have the phrases emerge gently from your heart rather than be a pounding insistence in your head. Hold each phrase in your attention, but don't hold onto the phrase too tightly.

I have thought of this practice as being rather like holding in my hand a fragile, precious object made of glass. If I were to grasp it too tightly, it would shatter and break. If I were to get lazy or negligent, it would fall from my hand and break. Connect to that object gently, with awareness. In just that way you can connect to, or cherish, each metta phrase.

Repeat the phrases with enough space and enough silence between so that they fall into a rhythm that is pleasing to you. Direct your attention to just one phrase at a time, knowing what it means. And each time you notice your attention has wandered, be kind to yourself and let go of the distraction. Come back to repeating the phrases without judging or disparaging yourself.

After some time of doing this, visual- **LISTEN TO CD TRACK 1**
ize yourself in the center of a circle. The Lovingkindness toward
circle is composed of those who have been ourselves
kind to you or have inspired you because
of their love. Perhaps you've met them, or read about them;
perhaps they live now, or they have existed historically or even
mythically. That is the circle. As you experience yourself in
the center of it, experience yourself as the recipient of their
love and attention. Keep gently repeating the phrases of lovingkindness for yourself.

To close the session, you can let go of the visualization and
simply keep repeating the phrases of metta for a few more
minutes. Each time you do so, you are transforming your old,
hurtful relationship to yourself and are moving forward sus-
tained by the force of kindness.

three

Overcoming Cruelty

The psychological root that empowers a natural sense of morality is the compassion that comes from empathy. Through the quality of empathy we understand that suffering hurts others in just the same way that it hurts us. This ability is what gives us an organic, straightforward sense of conscience. It reveals to us how likely it would be for someone to feel diminished if they were lied to, violated if they were stolen from, disempowered if they were excluded from a decision, desperate if they were hungry.

In Buddhist teachings, the image used to reflect this quality of mind is that of a feather held near a flame and the way it instantly curls away from the heat. In just that way, when

our minds become imbued with an understanding of how suffering feels and we are filled with a compassionate urge not to cause suffering in others, we naturally recoil from causing harm. This happens without self-consciousness or self-righteousness; it happens as a natural expression of the heart. We remember not to harm others because we actually understand how our actions could hurt them, as though it were our own bodies that could be injured, our own emotions set reeling, our own confidence broken. We see a piece of ourselves in them.

In contrast, if others are seen as objects rather than as feeling beings, it becomes quite easy to harm them, even in awful ways. Our lack of empathy reflects an inability to truly relate to other beings, to respect their boundaries, or to accept their feelings, their needs, their hopes, and dreams as viable, alive, and theirs. This is the misapprehension that allows a person to exploit and abuse others—and when it is extreme this is what allows us to be unkind without a care. More and more, we begin to view those we encounter mostly as likely competitors for the goodies we want, obstructions on our path to free enjoyment, potential challengers to our beliefs, and characters to be measured in light of the self-absorbed narrative we tell about our lives. From this vantage point we can objectify anyone. And once someone appears to us primarily as an object, kindness has no place to root.

When we experience the world dualistically, there is a pervasive sense of us and them, or self and other. Inevitably,

separation and distance are enhanced because of this duality. Instead of feeling intimacy with others—recognizing our shared wishes and vulnerabilities and our mutual dependence on one another—we resist. We put up "narrow, domestic walls," as poet Rabindranath Tagore termed them, and we cut ourselves off more and more. Sometimes those walls, that isolation, can come to feel like the most palpable, alive thing in our experience.

It's easy for us to feel separate from other people and from other forms of life, especially if we don't have a reliable connection to our own inner world. Without insight into our internal cycles of pleasure and pain, desires and fears, there is a strong sense of being removed, apart, or disconnected. When we do have an understanding of our inner lives, it provides an intuitive opening, even without words, to the ties that exist between ourselves and others.

The Buddha said that within this fathom-long body lies the entire universe. If we can understand our own experience and connect to it, we can connect to all of life, to the whole universe. We know that when we experience anger, it has a certain flavor and tone. We experience the pain of that anger, and we sense that it's not different from the pain other beings experience when angry. The causes may be completely different, the manifestations may be poles apart, one's sensitivity to how much it hurts may be blunted or exquisite, but the painful nature of anger holds true.

When we feel loved and seen for who we are, there is a liberating joy in that. It is distinctive and special, and we can know from clearly seeing love's spirit how enlivening it could be for others too. This is not to say we project our experience onto others or impose our views of what someone "must be" feeling, but rather that we can fathom, regardless of who is involved, states like the churning nature of mixed emotions, the hurt of being discounted, the relief of being cared about.

Without inner vision, it's easy to feel cut off and distant from others as though their experience is completely alien to our own. This is not only in terms of human beings—we might feel it even more so with other forms of life. If we live in this separated mode, if we constantly feel removed or alienated, we will develop a pervasive sense of self and other, with a very big "other" out there.

Upholding these divisions, the fundamental way we see the world is altered. Our commitments, our relationships, our sense of who belongs and who doesn't, who is "in" and who is "out," all change. We become more and more alone in a world we have created, a world where what we say or do to those who don't seem to matter doesn't count. Once a person fully becomes an object in our eyes, fully becomes the "other," we can do absolutely anything to them and the upholding of kindness dies.

I don't have to go through a litany here of the many different kinds of cruelty people are capable of. We are blasted by reports of horrifying behavior every day in the news. At times, we witness it tragically exhibited in our own families or communities. Sometimes those actions are just about beyond comprehension. At the time I was writing this in 2004, the world was watching the terrible events in South Asia, where it appeared that 150,000 people had died because of the tsunami hitting several countries. (Now the number of victims has increased significantly.)

Children were an estimated one-third of the death toll, and those who survived were suffering terribly. Thousands were orphaned, without anyone to protect them at first, and they were at great risk for starvation and disease. Shockingly, they were also reported to be in danger from human traffickers, who viewed the children as prey for the sex trade or as slaves.

I would watch television news coverage of the tsunami victims and see the haunted eyes of all those children who had lost their whole families—who were hungry, grieving, forlorn. I couldn't imagine how someone could view them as merchandise. Some days I visualized the perpetrators as ghosts flitting through life with nothing providing meaningful contact. I began to wonder if events and people and feelings were not

really palpable in their world, but only appeared as evasive shadows and fleeting impressions.

Or, I sometimes speculated, do they move implacably throughout the day as hardened as though they were shellacked, with nothing entering their defenses, nothing touching their hearts, with people and encounters bouncing off that solid armor? Whatever image came to me, I knew those children had to have been more like debris to them than like sorrowing, tender, frightened human beings.

When I consider people diluting chemotherapy drugs, robbing senior citizens, discriminating against those of another race, smacking kids, I inevitably think, "How in the world can they do that?" And then I pause and think again about the times I slice through someone's eagerness to connect with me with my indifference, my disregard, because I am not paying attention. I think about times I hold onto petty grievances and don't see the totality of the person I am resenting. I think about the times when I just don't care enough about the person in front of me, because I'm busy contemplating what I next will need from someone else.

We might not behave in a terrible fashion in any given moment because of our backgrounds or wisdom or circle of friends or sheer good luck, but we all know what it is like to look right through someone as though he or she weren't important. We all know what it is like to deny the vitality of someone's vulnerable, complex, mutable life once we have him or her nicely pigeonholed as the "other."

The Advaita Vedanta master H.W.L. Poonja once said in response to a question about bringing peace to the world, "As long as there are two, there will be war." As long as there is that insidious sense of self and other creating "two," and we can objectify that "other" for our own ends, there will be war in our hearts, in our families, in our neighborhoods, throughout the world.

Just as cruelty can ravage lives and trample hope, kindness can be the quality we choose to steer our lives by. Rabbi Abraham Heschel once talked about "a persistent effort to be worthy of the name 'human.'" We can't deny how much brutality and callousness humans are capable of. Yet at the same time, we can't deny the courage and compassion that offer us faith.

Kindness can provide the path to living in a different way. Poet Maya Angelou said, "If you find it in your heart to care for somebody else, you will have succeeded." Just as there are far too many instances of terrible cruelty and pain recklessly inflicted, there are wonderfully inspiring examples of how, sometimes against all odds, we can succeed in truly caring for somebody else.

A few years ago I was involved in the creation of a book, named *Sorrow Mountain*, the life story of Ani Pachen, a

Tibetan nun. Ani Pachen had been a princess in eastern Tibet and was the daughter of a local chieftain. When her father died, she replaced him in leading armies against the Chinese invaders. Eventually captured by the Chinese, she spent twenty-one years in prison undergoing beatings, deprivation, humiliation, and terrible loneliness. Throughout her ordeal, Ani Pachen used meditation practice and whatever she knew of Buddhist teachings to survive. Once she was released, she escaped to India and became a nun.

My friend Daidie Donnelly was writing *Sorrow Mountain*, and to provide Daidie with the biographical material she would need, we brought Ani to the United States for a series of taped interviews. At one point on that trip Ani was staying at my house in Barre, Massachusetts.

That whole period of time was a difficult one for her. Answering Daidie's questions inevitably brought up piercing memories of Ani's difficult past, and to some extent she was reliving it all. One morning as we had breakfast together, I was struck by how solicitous Ani was of the rest of us. "Do you want some toast? Do you need some more tea?"

It didn't seem like she was putting on the polite facade people sometimes assume to carefully divert everyone's attention, even their own, from a confrontation with their pain. Rather, it seemed like a genuine caring about others' comfort and ease. I looked at Ani across the breakfast table and thought, "Wow, if I had spent twenty-one years in prison, I don't know if I

would come out with nearly enough energy left over from my own bitterness to be worried about someone else's supply of tea and toast in the morning." And yet, we can.

How to have strength of heart when we have confronted cruelty directly or indirectly? One of the terrible things about experiencing the cruelty that can flow from others toward us—whether through racism or sexism, through being dismissed as secondary, or through any of the varied ways we might be categorized, filed away, and ignored by someone—is the way it grinds us down. It is all too easy to begin believing this projected image of ourselves as someone not worth much—and to take that in and begin to live from that reflection as though it were true. To get back in touch with kindness is to get back in touch with our own bigger, vibrant, more expansive potential instead of being defined by the limited, biased vision others put upon us. Why see ourselves through the distortion of their particular lens?

Even if others don't intend to harm us, their careless disregard or easy assumptions about us can be demeaning. There's a story that I've always enjoyed from the time of the Buddha about a nun named Citta who was very elderly when she first entered the order of nuns and began her meditation practice.

Many of the other nuns and monks would say to her, "You know, you're really old; you should just take it easy. Just slow down, relax, and don't try to practice very much. Have a nice vacation as a nun for this last period of your life."

But Citta had tremendous motivation for freedom, and she thought, "No, I really want to meditate," even though so many people told her she should give up the aspiration.

One day, despite the comments from others urging hesitation, Citta decided to walk up a mountain. While walking, she said to herself, "At the end of this day either the hindrances to enlightenment will have died, or I'll have died."

She walked up the mountain, spent time on top meditating, and as these stories always end so happily, she became fully enlightened. Then she proceeded to walk back down. At the bottom, it is said that the whole community gathered around her and exclaimed, "You look really good, what happened to you?"

We are all too often told by someone that we are too old, too young, too different, too much the same—and those comments can be devastating. Any of us might recall being misunderstood, overlooked, abandoned, treated unjustly. When we succumb to this we belong to others and are in exile from ourselves. To return to ourselves we have to be in touch with what we fundamentally care about, that which allows us to know who we are.

A dedication to kindness offers us a chance to try to make a real difference despite the obstacles and unhappiness we might face. No matter what our belief system, actions, or status, we are joined together in this world through strands of relationship and interconnection. That suffering child, orphaned through a tsunami, who we see in Indonesia or Sri Lanka is part of our own lives, and we must not forget that. There is nothing that just happens only "there" anymore—not a war, not an exploitation of the weak, not a disease, not a hope for change. We need to stop reinforcing the sense of dehumanization, of "us" and "them," of separation that leads to wanton cruelty in the first place.

And if tomorrow is going to look any better than today, we must realize that the currency for compassion isn't what someone does, right or wrong—it is the very fact that that person exists. Commitment to the possibility of kindness cannot be discarded as foolish or irrelevant, even in troubling times when we often can't find easy answers. If we abandon the force of kindness as we confront cruelty, we won't learn anything to take into tomorrow—not from history, not from one another, not from life.

Even if we are encountering cruelty, we must try to understand its roots and determine not to be the same as those

acting it out. We must determine not to simply keep perpetrating the forces of separation and disregard. If we don't make that effort, what will we really have accomplished?

One of my exemplars in this way is Aung San Suu Kyi, leader of the pro-democracy movement in Burma. In 1989 Suu Kyi was placed under house arrest for her political activities. While still confined, she received the Nobel Peace Prize in 1991. At the time of her arrest, Suu Kyi's sons were sixteen and twelve, and she was unable to see them again for years. It was more than two years before she saw her husband again.

Describing her imprisonment, Suu Kyi wrote, "I refused to accept anything from the military. Sometimes I didn't even have enough money to eat. I became so weak from malnourishment that my hair fell out, and I couldn't get out of bed."

During that time, Aung San Suu Kyi was involved in the practice of metta, or lovingkindness meditation. Despite the suffering of her situation, she later said, "When I compared notes with my colleagues in the democracy movement in Burma who have suffered long terms of imprisonment, we found that an enhanced appreciation of metta was a common experience. We had known and felt both the effects of lovingkindness and the unwholesomeness of natures lacking in lovingkindness."

Can you imagine having your whole life turned upside down and suffering so intensely, yet still having the presence of mind to realize that those who have hurt you are acting from an objectification of you? To be able to see that they are

acting from a profound ignorance of who you are that you don't want in any way to replicate? Can you imagine seeking strength without hatred, power without vengefulness, authority without dualism and division? Can you imagine having that much openness, that much courage, and that much imagination itself?

Today Suu Kyi is still in Burma, still under house arrest. Her children have grown up without her; her husband died without being permitted to enter the country to say goodbye. Her steadfast practice in the face of terrible adversity might be summed up in this quotation from her: "A saint is a sinner who keeps on trying."

We can all keep on trying, through the extension of lovingkindness to others, and make the effort to pay attention to them in an inclusive way rather than splitting them off into the "other"—the "different" ones who can be hurt with impunity. This doesn't at all mean that we will like everybody or acquiesce to everything that he or she does. It doesn't mean that we become complacent or passive about naming wrongdoing as wrong or about seeking change, sometimes very forcefully, with our whole heart.

Practicing lovingkindness does mean that we learn to see the lives of others, really see them, as related to our own lives. It means that we open up to the possibility of caring for others not just because we like them or admire them or are indebted to them in some way, but because our lives are inextricably

linked to one another's. We use the practice of lovingkindness meditation as a way to recover our innermost knowledge of that linkage as we dissolve the barriers we have been upholding and genuinely awaken to how connected we all are.

Ways to Offer Lovingkindness to Others
- Reflect on a time you have been objectified by someone. What were the consequences? Reflect on a time you have objectified someone else. What were the consequences?
- Take the time to pay attention to a stranger—someone you pass on the street or see in the subway. As an exercise, imagine where they are going and what their day will be like.
- Stay aware of the internal feelings generated when someone hurts you through his or her own unskillful actions. Remember that this is what others feel as well when they are hurt or harmed.
- Stay aware of the internal feelings generated when someone gives you a gift or is kind to you. Remember that this is what others feel as well.
- Pay full attention and really look at and listen to someone you usually ignore or find annoying.
- Practice lovingkindness meditation toward others as well as yourself.

MEDITATION

Lovingkindness toward Others

Moving on from offering lovingkindness to ourselves, we practice offering lovingkindness to others. Using the same metta phrases we have practiced with ourselves, we focus on offering lovingkindness to others in an expanding arc of relationships. With each person, see if you can bring an image of them to mind or feel their presence as though they were right in front of you. Say their name to yourself, and offer the phrases of lovingkindness to them, focusing on one phrase at a time. Don't struggle to fabricate a feeling or sentiment. And when you have found that your mind has wandered, simply begin again.

- May you live in safety.
- May you have mental happiness (peace, joy).
- May you have physical happiness (health, freedom from pain).
- May you live with ease. (May the elements of daily life—work, family—go easily, not be a struggle.)

We begin with someone who has been of help to us. This person, known as a benefactor, may be someone who has directly been generous or kind to us or perhaps has inspired us even though we have never met him or her. He or she is the one who, when we think of that person, makes us smile.

After a few minutes, move on to a friend. You can start with a friend who is doing well right now, enjoying success or joy

in some aspect of life. Then switch to a friend who is having difficulty right now, experiencing loss or pain or unhappiness.

Next, we offer metta to a neutral person, someone we don't feel a strong liking or disliking for. Sometimes people find that there are very few neutral people in their lives; as soon as they meet someone they tend to form a judgment of them. Sometimes people find that there are too many neutral people in their lives; outside a certain favored circle, people might as well be pieces of furniture for all the care we have for them.

Often these are people who perform a certain function in our lives: the checkout person in the supermarket, the bank teller, the dry cleaner. When we choose a neutral person and offer them metta, we are offering it to them simply on the basis that they exist—we are not terribly indebted to them or challenged by them. Because we share this planet and this life, we include them in our care as well.

- May you live in safety.
- May you have mental happiness (peace, joy).
- May you have physical happiness (health, freedom from pain).
- May you live with ease. (May the elements of daily life— work, family—go easily, not be a struggle.)

Following this period, we begin working with metta toward a person with whom we have conflict or difficulty. We usually begin with someone only mildly difficult and then slowly work toward sending metta to someone who has hurt us more

grievously. It is common to feel resentment and anger toward the difficult person . . . and important not to judge ourselves for that. Rather, we recognize that our anger burns within our own hearts and causes us suffering, so out of the greatest respect and compassion for ourselves we practice letting go and offering metta.

It is also important to realize that by offering metta to a difficult person we are not condoning their actions and trying to pretend it doesn't matter that they have hurt us or someone else. It does matter, and we need to acknowledge that. Instead of practicing denial, we are seeing deeply into our hearts and discovering a capacity for lovingkindness that is intelligent and wise—that lifts us out of old dynamics and frees us from dependence on circumstances and personalities in defining our priorities. Of course this part of the practice is as challenging as it is liberating.

If even a mildly difficult person arouses too much resentment, go back to offering lovingkindness to yourself. This isn't secondary or remedial practice in some way; the development of greater love and compassion for ourselves is the essential foundation for being able to offer metta to others.

We finish the meditation by offering lovingkindness in a spontaneous way to anyone who comes to mind—people, animals, those whom we like, those whom we don't, in an adventurous expanse of our own power of kindness.

LISTEN TO CD TRACK 2
Lovingkindness toward others

47

four

How We See the World

In talking about suffering, what causes it, the chance we each have to come out of it, and the way to do that, the Buddha's teaching is never removed from a sense of humanity. The Buddha himself, as a human being, ultimately was talking about what it means to be a human being and to be happy—in a radical sense of happiness. The teachings honor and respect the possibility of happiness so that the idea of achieving it is not something tinged with fear or shame or squeamishness, as in our common plaint, "Oh, I don't know if I deserve to be happy."

The Buddhist belief is that everyone at heart wants to be happy, that we should be happy, and that in fact we can be happy as human beings in complex, real, tumultuous lives.

Everyone longs, at heart, for a feeling of being at home in this body and mind, in this life. We all want to feel a part of something greater than our limited sense of self. If we look carefully at any action—even a powerful, unwholesome action— we can sense that within there's an urge to feel less separated, to find an elusive form of happiness, to find a sense of uniting. Even if we look at addictive or violent behavior, at the root we sense an urge to feel something different, significant, real.

The basic wish for happiness is constructive and within all of us—even if it manifests in terrible and damaging ways because of the ignorance that distorts that wish, and even if it leads us to look for happiness where it will never be found. If the wish for happiness can be aligned with wisdom instead of ignorance, that urge becomes our homing instinct for freedom, allowing us to cut through many obstacles.

But one of the first things we need to do is to be honest about the pain.

We acknowledge our pain, not to get more depressed or to drown in the suffering, but to see the truth of our experience—not just the superficial truth of passing circumstance, but the deeper underlying truth. Looking into the heart of pain, we feel joined to others. We see that while everyone wants to be happy, we are all vulnerable as life moves and shifts and stirs all of the time. We see that our lives can transform in an instant to something unrecognizable from what we anticipated when we woke up this morning and began the day.

This is true for all of us, all of the time. This recognition lifts us up and leads us to compassion and its unique happiness, which is connection.

It's easy to be unconscious. It takes something very compelling to turn us around, to turn us away from all the easy, complacent answers society offers us about how to live. This is what the story of the Buddha's life is about. It is said that there was a prophecy at the time of Prince Siddhartha's (later the Buddha) birth saying that there were two possible ways for him to go in his life. One was for him to become a world-reigning monarch and the other was for him to become an awakened one—a Buddha. On hearing this, his father, who wanted his child to be a monarch, decided that he was going to protect him from ever having to see anything unpleasant. In this way, the young prince would just enjoy his life and not be moved to question more deeply.

The legend says that it was at the age of twenty-nine when the prince actually left the palace grounds and saw, for the first time, an old person, a sick person, a corpse, and then a renunciant—which was his call to awakening. He set out to seek a truth of happiness that would stand the tests of time, of change, of sickness, of loss.

Opening to our own suffering can lead us to try to seek a better way, a more meaningful life, and a deeper understanding. It's like a call to awakening to not spend our lives defined by someone else's determination of what our limits are, to not

mindlessly live out the conventional understandings. It propels us to comprehend what lies behind the closed doors of others' lives, to be willing to see their joys and their sorrows, and to be motivated by a powerful commitment to support the highest possible happiness for them and for us. Opening to suffering wakes us up to compassion and kindness.

Compassion is defined in Buddhist teaching as the trembling or quivering of the heart in response to seeing pain or suffering. Along with love and altruism, compassion can be seen as warmheartedness replacing cynicism, beneficence taking the place of indifference, caring supplanting aloofness. These qualities strip away rigid divisions between us and invite us to take another look at ourselves and at the world around us.

One key to the development of compassion seems to be in learning how to step out of our normal habit patterns in connection to our pain. Forging the right relationship to pain is very complex, because suffering can be a tremendously powerful teacher and an opening. But as we know, it can also be the cause of terrible anger and separation, in a multitude of forms. We can be filled with loneliness and antagonism because we're in pain. We can feel a lot of guilt when in a state of grief, condemning ourselves for something we did or something we didn't do or something we didn't say. We can feel cut off from and resentful of those reaching out to us, because we're hurting and they don't seem to be. And we certainly can blame

ourselves for being weak and inadequate when we try to make a difference in a world that needs so much help.

Any degree of suffering can be experienced as overwhelming, a sealed room from which we see no protruding edge to provide a toehold and facilitate escape. Compassion gives us that toehold, allowing us to use our own pain and our witness of the pain of others as a vehicle for connection rather than isolation. It allows us to open rather than close down, to have an entirely different understanding of the possibility of a special kind of happiness, even in painful and challenging times, and of the role kindness plays in realizing it.

I had an illustration of the possibility of experiencing happiness in the midst of challenge in the summer of 1999. The Dalai Lama had come to New York City for several days of teaching at a rented venue, followed by a large public talk in Central Park. Entering the park on the morning of the public talk, I at first didn't see the crowd, but I could hear the sound of Tibetan monks chanting in the distance. Walking toward the sound, I finally turned a corner and was stunned to see a veritable ocean of people. Everywhere the eye could land there were people, gathered to hear the Dalai Lama. Some estimates had the crowd at 250,000.

We sat in an unusual kind of quiet for so large a number, waiting for the Dalai Lama to begin speaking. And when he did begin, he began with a statement I found startling. He said, "In many ways, it hasn't been such an easy life." He went on to describe how he had to assume temporal power at the age of sixteen, flee into exile in his early twenties, daily try to keep a culture in exile intact, daily hear of the devastation and suffering going on inside Tibet. "In many ways it hasn't been such an easy life." Indeed.

Then abruptly he giggled and said, "But I'm pretty happy." And of course this is what one sees in him. Despite his burdens, he doesn't seem weighed down, morose, or hopeless. And clearly this isn't a conventional kind of happiness, the fragile joy of getting what we want until it shifts, or being able to hold tightly onto something for a while as a totem against change or death. It's a different quality altogether, a quality sustainable in varied life circumstances, pleasant or painful. He continued, "The reason I am pretty happy is because of the force of compassion. Compassion makes me feel at one with everyone."

The Dalai Lama's statement was particularly striking because of the 250,000 or so of us sitting there. I bet a lot of us could have said, "It hasn't been such an easy life." But not too many of us could have followed that with, "But I'm pretty happy!" This is the transformative power of compassion, which can directly experience unhappiness and yet have kindness born from it.

Compassion reveals familiar barriers like disdain, enmity, and division to be constructs built by culture or custom or personal needs or fears—but not necessarily fixed in stone, inevitable, or inherent in our being. How much better it is to feel at one with everyone, even if life is hard, than to be embroiled in bitterness, or for us to decide that it is better to be without friends because we think we cannot afford to care for anyone else.

When we see how quickly life just disappears, how even the longest life span is over in a flash, we realize how important it is for us to create the conditions that help us most quickly, most directly, and most strongly move toward true happiness. The bravest thing we can do, and the beginning of an awakened life—a life suffused with kindness—is to question our assumptions about what we are capable of, what brings us happiness, and what life can be about.

Many factors may make the development of kindness challenging. We may feel competitive and find within a tad of satisfaction when someone is a little down, so that we can feel superior. We might genuinely care but are afraid of getting involved. We might find ourselves dominated by a feeling of helplessness or a sense that anything at all we could offer would be horribly insufficient. We might be confused as to the right thing to do.

If we are willing to take a risk anyway and consciously practice kindness, we see that, unlike the world's messages—"Buy more,"

"Compete more strongly," "It's a dog-eat-dog world"—a much more refined happiness comes from feeling joined, from a sense of belonging—both to this life and to one another. We need to hone our own sense of purpose. We need to understand what will actually allow happiness beyond acquisition, what will help us realize happiness more steadfast than any temporary pleasure or fleeting triumph.

In talking about happiness, what causes it and how to practice those causes to genuinely achieve it, everything that the Buddha taught is rooted in simplicity and leads to liberation.

First we look at our vision of life and of ourselves in relation to one another. This is something that is not in any way fixed or determined, but that can grow and expand all the time as we perceive things more acutely or see them from a different angle. I noticed this several years ago, when I was quite sick all winter. I had bronchitis, and every time I began to get better I'd have a relapse. Finally I actually began to recover.

I was living in New York City at the time, and while walking down the street one day I heard a woman's voice saying, "I was very sick all winter." Naturally intrigued, I turned around and saw a woman handing a street person, who was sitting on the sidewalk, some money. She went on talking to him: "I

had pneumonia, and every time I started to get better I'd have a relapse. Now I am finally really getting better, and I just wanted to share the joy."

I was taken aback. Realizing that I had just walked right by that man without a thought of sharing the joy of my own renewed health, I wondered if I should approach him, hand him more money, and say, "You won't believe this, but I was really sick all winter too, and I'd like to share some joy as well."

I ended up not doing that, but I felt I learned something from that woman. The decision of whether or not to give a street person some money is a complex one, based on many considerations, and there is not one right answer to suit every situation. What made this such a forceful lesson for me was the fact that I had walked right past that man without the thought that his life had something to do with my own. Without that view, there was no impetus to relate to him in any way—either through noticing his sorrow or thinking for a moment of sharing my own joy.

Life can and does turn on a dime. One little rotation of the wheel of fortune and we ourselves are not feeling so on top of life and impervious to change. Kindness doesn't say, "I, who have everything together and am invulnerable, am standing way over here looking at you poor thing way over there, and since our lives don't touch except in this tiny, peripheral way at this moment, I am going to just toss you some money."

With insight we see that we all share the urge toward happiness, and also that no one leaves this earth without having suffered. Thus we look at others and see something not only about them, but about ourselves.

Often this insight extends only so far until we hit a wall, but then something may happen—a confrontation, a new relationship, a dawning view of the intricacy of a person's life—and we find our perspective broadening. A friend of mine was a wonderfully empathic therapist. One day a man came to see her, beseeching her to be his therapist. She found his political views alienating, his feelings about women difficult, and his behavior quite annoying. In short, she didn't like him and urged him to find another therapist. However, because he very much wanted to work with her, she finally acquiesced and took him on as a client.

Now, because he was her client, she tried to look with compassion instead of disdain or repugnance at his unskillful behavior and all the ways he shut himself off. She began to see all the ways in which his life was very difficult. Soon, even though she continued to see, without denial, his unpleasant behavior, she found herself doing so with the feeling that she was necessarily his ally. The goal became his release from suffering, which would also affect those around him. As she put it, he had become "hers." Even though I don't believe she ever came to like him or approve of many of his views, she came to care about him.

Hearing this story from my friend, I began to think of the role of the *bodhisattva.* In the Buddhist tradition, a bodhisattva is one who aspires to enlightenment, dedicating her or his transformed mind and actions to the liberation of all beings. When we aspire to be a bodhisattva, everyone becomes "ours" in a way. Our goal becomes the release from suffering of all beings, and so we view ourselves as working on behalf of everyone. Even when we take very strong steps toward keeping someone from acting as harmfully as they may be acting, we do this to the best of our ability without rancor or contempt. Developing more of this perspective is a great challenge, and it is also a great opportunity for the unique happiness compassion can offer.

One word for kindheartedness or compassion in the Pali language is *anukampa*, which means being moved in response to others, having a tender mind or an open heart. Developing a deepening kindheartedness or tenderness doesn't mean that we consign someone else to a fixed role as "the unfortunate one," as though to say we are perfectly fine and always will be, while they, cast down as they are, have nothing at all they can give to us at this point in time, and never will. There is often a strong mutuality in acts of kindness, so that many hospice aides, literacy tutors, volunteers working to provide meals to

ill people with AIDS, and others engaged in helping of all kinds have told me unequivocally that through those actions they invariably get much more than they give.

Compassion also doesn't imply that we define someone solely in terms of their victimhood, their incapacity, or their troubles, as though they were nothing more than that designation and therefore even further removed from us and our own lives. Zainab Salbi, founder of Women for Women International, an organization helping women on the front lines in many war-torn countries, made reference to this when she spoke at the 2005 Sacred Circles conference at the National Cathedral in Washington D.C. Zainab spoke about a time when she repeatedly referred to a woman from such a country in terms of her having been raped, only to realize later, to her dismay, that she had not recounted in addition the fact that the woman was a lawyer.

When we forget the complexity of a life, we also forget to look at what is whole in a person—what is intact and vital and generative. With the force of kindness, we can look at someone else and see those things as well as his or her pain. This helps us look at ourselves and see those same things within, alongside seeing our own pain. Then compassion and kindness connect us to a bigger picture of life where we can see pain but also love, loss but also movement, sorrow but also togetherness.

This is an immense vision, one that is made real through our practice of lovingkindness for all of life without exception. At

a fundamental level, our connectedness to others is expressed by our wish for the welfare of all, our dedication to their happiness, safety, and peace. This is how we consciously remember what our lives are about. If we follow this inspiration through our practice, then we can carry it into our everyday interactions, encounters, and relationships.

We practice this value by connecting to the boundlessness of life and offering metta to all beings everywhere—all beings, all creatures, all individuals, all those in existence. We realize that everyone wants to be happy just as we ourselves do. All suffer, all know longing and being thwarted, all undergo change and will eventually die just as in the turning of the seasons. Using the quality of compassion as a springboard, we open our minds and develop the ability to include instead of exclude, to pay attention to rather than ignore someone.

Instead of relegating anybody to the classification of "irrelevant to my life," we realize the interdependence of all of existence. Whether someone is known to us or unknown to us, near or far, female or male, wise or ignorant, cruel or kind, she or he is part of this greater fabric of life itself, and we recognize our essential interrelatedness.

Remember, this doesn't mean that we approve of everyone, or that we won't fight hard to rectify injustice or challenge harmful behavior. Instead, we use the power of our attention to open rather than to remain shut down, and in that openness we see life as it is: connected to us in its entirety,

containing all facets and aspects of existence and experience, not disparate or fragmented or severed from us but as a whole.

Over time, offering lovingkindness to all beings everywhere, including ourselves, unites us to one another so that we know we cannot go forward forgetting those left behind. We cannot achieve true happiness in a vacuum of egotism. We cannot experience true happiness without the development of kindness and compassion.

Ways to Bring Kindness to All

- Before a meal, take a moment and reflect on those far-flung people involved in your enjoying that meal—the people who grew the food and the people who transported it, stored it, and prepared it.
- Before a meal, reflect on the earth and the sun and the rain and all that nourished that food so it could nourish you.
- Think of a friend or family member who is difficult, but whom you love anyway. Examine the dynamics of that relationship and how we might care for someone and still honestly see the difficulty.
- Stay open to surprise. Roles and relationships are constantly changing. Reflect on how we go up and we go down all of the time.
- Pay attention as you are offering help to someone. What emotional or spiritual benefits are coming to you in return?
- Practice lovingkindness meditation for all beings.

MEDITATION
Lovingkindness for All Beings
First we offer the phrases of lovingkindness to different categories of beings, making sure to include pairs of opposites or complementary sets, so that taken together they form the whole of life.

Here are the kinds of phrases you might use:
  • May you live in safety.
  • May you have mental happiness (peace, joy).
  • May you have physical happiness (health, freedom from pain).
  • May you live with ease. (May the elements of daily life—work, family—go easily, not be a struggle.)

And here are the traditional categories to whom you might offer the phrases:
  • All females, and then all males
  • All enlightened beings, and then all unenlightened beings
  • All those whose lives are largely happy
  • All those whose lives are a mixture of pleasure and pain
  • All those whose lives are largely painful

We can use those categories or any others that may come to mind, as long as, when combined, they cover a big picture of life. Of course, we may be partial to one side of things. In other words, we may like enlightened beings a whole lot more

than we like unenlightened beings, but the exercise works to gently dissolve our reluctance to include someone each time we spend a few minutes offering the phrases of lovingkindness beyond our preferences.

We gently repeat the phrases, focusing on one at a time. If there are no waves of emotion or sentiment, don't worry about it. The practice is developed through the power of concentration we are building. If you find your attention has wandered, see if you can gather your energy, let go of the distraction without judgment, and come back to the phrases.

We then move on to offer these phrases to all beings everywhere, without distinction, as an expression of our capacity to connect to and care for all of life. We offer the phrases of lovingkindness to all beings in a variety of ways, directing them to "all beings, all creatures, all individuals, all those in existence."

LISTEN TO CD TRACK 3
Lovingkindness for
all beings

In part, the practice is done by going through different categories that essentially mean the same thing simply for the poetry of it. In addition, these different expressions of an expansive view of life, though identical on one level, each offer a slightly different picture and sensibility in the unfolding of the meditation. They each serve to open our hearts.

five

Ethics and Kindness

A friend of mine, at the end of a retreat, offered a provocative reflection that intrigued and inspired me. After looking intensively at her inner experience for nine days of meditation and seeing many of her life choices in a brand new light, she commented, "If you really want to be a rebel, practice kindness."

There could be many wonderful extrapolations: "If you really want to be outrageous, be ethical." "If you want to go against the grain, be kindhearted." "If you want to live on your own terms, breaking out from expectations and external demands, practice love." "To be free, to be different, to be bold, be compassionate."

My friend is an independent thinker, a person who likes to make her own decisions and set her own goals. She likes to know what options she has before her and to be able to choose the one that is individual, distinctive, nonconformist. When she can really be herself and not assume a facade in order to please people or fit in or meet their expectations, she is happy. I think she was absolutely right about kindness and rebellion.

The world may tell us to grab as much as we want, and we might think that the audacity of rebelliousness is to grab even more with impunity, but how about being really radical and questioning how much we need? Conventional wisdom may be that retribution displays strength and can summarily bring an end to conflicts, but how about taking a leap and challenging ourselves to a whole new meaning of resolution based on mutuality and caring? The easy way may be to turn away and distract ourselves from the distress and suffering of others, but how about being daring enough to pay attention? Our conditioning may tell us we don't need anybody, but how about taking a real look at life and noticing that we are all entwined in a fabric of interdependence—then being willing to risk acting accordingly?

Although in current times there are some common connotations of morality, such as prudishness or expressing fear of life, in fact a commitment to ethics is a commitment to living life in the most free, most loving, most expansive sense. In Buddhist teaching, morality does not mean a forced or

puritanical abiding by rules. Morality means living with intentions that reflect our love and compassion for ourselves as well as our caring for others. As the philosopher George Santayana said, "Morality is the desire to lessen suffering in the world." Living in a way that doesn't perpetuate hurting ourselves or hurting another is considered to be an expression both of great power and great compassion.

The Buddha said that if we truly loved ourselves we would never harm another, because if we harm another it in some way diminishes who we are. There is no way to emerge undamaged ourselves when we lash out at someone physically or verbally, belittle their achievements, exploit them in some way, or consider them unworthy of hearing the truth. We are capable of so much more, and we dishonor that potential when we don't live with integrity.

The Buddha also said, "When watching after oneself, one watches after others. When watching after others, one watches after oneself." And he went on to question, "How does one, by watching after oneself, watch after others?" By sustaining meditation and having access to our inner world of thoughts and feelings, we can more and more understand our deeper motivations, and we can also begin to catch sight of our fleeting impulses. We come to understand how to form a meaningful aspiration for our lives, and we learn how to be in touch with that aspiration in different and challenging circumstances.

We also learn increasingly how to let go of distractions, to stay more grounded when facing the lure of addictions, and to remember to take a calming breath instead of acting out in a flash of anger. Because of these insights and skills, we can watch after or take care of others by taking care of ourselves.

"And how does one, when watching after others, watch after oneself?" By cultivating patience. By practicing harmlessness. By the power of love. By the condition of tender care. When we are dedicated to relating to others in these ways, we are taking care of ourselves and them because we are focusing our lives. We are not just being tossed around by circumstances that arise and pass away outside of our control.

When we are committed to an ethical life, we are not ruled by changing conditions in the outside world. We have a thread of meaning in our lives; we have a sense of dedication that reflects great love for ourselves and a deeper understanding of where happiness is to be found. If we take care of others we find that our self-respect grows and flourishes, and that this is the basis for our growing confidence, courage, and ease of heart.

We don't need any sort of religious orientation to lead a life that is ethical, compassionate, and kind. It is, as the Dalai

Lama puts it so aptly, a case of "enlightened self-interest." If we really want to be happy, to be life-affirming, to be free of the tiresome and binding constraints of what is ordinary and merely habitual, we should look at the force of kindness as it is lived through morality.

When we don't follow through on a momentary impulse to do a harmful act, we are more able to see the impermanence and the transparency of the desire or anger that arose to fuel that action to begin with. Even if they come up strongly, we are empowered by our ability to choose not to act from a place of desire or anger or anxiety. We see that we need not be afraid of those impulses any longer, while at the same time we can choose not to follow their call. We can make the choice to let go of harmful urges without any rancor toward ourselves— or any shame about what we might be feeling or fearing or wanting—but instead out of the greatest love for ourselves.

Having avoided harmful action, we also avoid the guilt, fear of discovery, confusion, and regret that come when we forget that what we do and say has consequences. Because we do fewer actions that keep us feeling separate from others, the common, dispiriting sense of loneliness and alienation we can have is relieved. We find greater lightness and ease in our lives as we increasingly care for ourselves and other beings.

More and more we experience the happiness of composure and strength. Rather than the turbulence and agitation that we undergo when our minds are full of worry, remorse, and

guilt, we find that we more easily experience inner quietude. Because there is not a great bundle of complexity that we are creating—one that we may subsequently need to disentangle and try somehow to make amends for—we can be more peaceful in this moment.

This is a quality of happiness that is not going to fracture as conditions change, when people behave in disappointing ways, or when we do not get what we want. This is a kind of happiness based on knowing our interconnectedness, on the integrity of acting from our deepest values. This is the practice of learning how to truly be a friend to ourselves and others. And this is the understanding that being a friend to ourselves and being a friend to others is really the same thing.

The Buddha often spoke with a tremendous pragmatism, which is reflective of the force of his compassion. His teaching isn't lofty, abstract, or removed from people; it is very present, very available. To describe the qualities of an ethical life, the Buddha often emphasized the characteristics of a good friend. He spoke about a good friend—a true friend—as being someone who is a helper, who will protect us when we are taken unawares, when we are surprised by life in some way. This person will be a refuge to us when we're afraid. He spoke about a good friend as

someone who is constant in our times of happiness and in our times of adversity or sorrow, someone who will not forsake us when we're in trouble. A true friend is someone who will tell us their secrets and will not betray our secrets to others, while also being completely honest with us and warning us if he or she thinks we are heading toward danger.

The Buddha talked about this kind of friend as being someone who is sympathetic, declaring that this is not a person who will rejoice over our misfortune. A true friend actually takes delight when things are going well for us and when we're happy, rather than being envious or jealous. She or he will try to stop someone when that person is speaking ill of us and will praise those who speak well of us. A good friend exemplifies qualities like generosity and morality and balance. When we have such a friend, we have a gift beyond measure. And not only can we appreciate the true friends we have, we can determine to be a good friend to others—and not just to a precious few we owe a favor to, or only to those whom we love personally and uniquely. We can determine to approach life as a whole in that way.

In this light, the Buddha exhorted his students to make their lives count, both for themselves and for the protection of all

71

beings. No matter how one is living—whether alone or in partnership, whether raising children or not, whether mostly in solitude or in a large public forum—it is important to have our lives be an expression of all that we know and all that we care about. In fact, this unity of wisdom and compassion empowers our commitment to an awakened life, one where we can see things clearly and respond skillfully.

In the Buddhist teaching, the gift of morality is considered the gift of fearlessness. The commitment to not harming allows us to be worthy of trust from others—they know they have nothing to fear from us. They know we'll be straightforward and forthright—they won't have to look for veiled messages and disguised insults. We won't try to feel better about ourselves by attempting to take away from what they have. And we won't take advantage of them to our own ends, without regard to the consequences for them.

With a growing commitment to morality we are able to live in a state of greater fearlessness ourselves. We won't have the divisiveness that comes from having a secret life. We won't have the disorder in our minds of not quite remembering how we might have shaded the truth, and to whom. We won't have the weight in our hearts of dreading the potential results of our actions. So much of our energy, once tied up in hiding the truth from ourselves or from others, is freed and becomes available to us. To develop a heart that is untroubled, that's free from anxiety, is to develop a heart that is vast, unconfined, and measureless.

There is no one model of behavior that is the perfect expression of sympathy and concern and compassion, but we have the classic five precepts of the Buddhist tradition as a guideline for living a lay life in the world. The first precept is to refrain from killing any living being. Based on our interconnectedness to all beings, this commitment develops a reverence in us for all of life. The next precept is to refrain from stealing or taking that which has not been offered. If we practice care in this way, we develop a deep sense of contentment. The third precept, to refrain from sexual misconduct, means refraining from using our sexual energy in a way that causes harm to ourselves or to others. Often so much sheer recklessness propels us, followed by very strong regret, because we haven't taken the time to look at the likely consequences of acting out a particular desire.

The fourth precept is to refrain from lying and inappropriate speech, which acknowledges the power and impact of how we communicate. Many times harmony and trust are destroyed because of mere words, ephemeral as they might seem. And the last of the five basic precepts is to refrain from taking intoxicants such as drugs or alcohol, which cloud the mind and cause heedlessness, preventing us from experiencing the power of our mind in its natural state.

These precepts essentially provide a foundation for a life of awareness. They are not intended to be put forth as draconian laws. The teaching of morality is not considered a

heavy burden that one must assume to be a righteous person. Undertaking a greater adherence to the precepts is like going on an adventure—being willing to take a risk and daring to be different in the direction of greater morality. That is rare in this world, where we often confuse compassion with timidity and restraint with inhibition.

Once when I was in Burma, someone asked my teacher, Sayadaw U Pandita, about that last precept—refraining from using intoxicants that cloud the mind and cause heedlessness. There are several interpretations of this precept, some coming down on the side of moderation being okay but not excess, others saying that using any alcohol or recreational drug at all is to break the precept. I suspected from the tone of voice of the questioner that he was hoping for Sayadaw U Pandita to recommend moderation, in which case he could happily go on having his occasional beer.

Instead, Sayadaw said, "There is one way you can have a drink and it would not be breaking the precept—that is if someone tied you up, poured the drink down your throat, *and* you didn't enjoy it." The questioner was crestfallen, and I was highly amused. I found it something of an extreme response and was somewhat flippant in my mind about it. Then I paused and thought, "Why dismiss this interpretation out of hand? Why not try not drinking at all for six months?"

I wasn't in the habit of drinking much anyway, but I resolved to drink nothing at all for a few months to see if it

made any difference in my life. To my surprise, I found that it did. I felt a greater clarity and strength of mind. I felt a greater solidarity with my friends who were recovering from addiction and who every day faced our society's appeals to let loose and indulge. I was so glad I was willing to make an experiment in the direction of greater simplicity, more calm, and less license. How often are we encouraged to do that? It is a radical act in our world.

Abiding by the precepts allows our lives to be seamless, rather than fragmented, espousing truth but lying anyway, or admiring friendship as a concept but stabbing someone behind their backs. We bring our lives together into an integrated whole. We may not find paying attention to how we speak to one another or questioning how we live with our families or how we relate to people at work too spiritually inspiring. Perhaps we'd much rather focus on a great transcendent state of consciousness out there somewhere, waiting for us to achieve it. But it is in how we live day to day that an authentic spirituality is made manifest.

When we undertake a path, it's not always easy. To have a sense of morality, for example, is not always easy because life is complicated and relationships are complicated. Sometimes telling a lie seems kinder, or we feel caught between competing pressures and can't figure out which way of acting causes less harm. For example, when termites are invading our house, do we exterminate them? There may be many times and many

situations when we simply don't know what the right thing is to do. But that is the process of waking up and trying to live consciously instead of mechanically. If we have a sense of what our path is, we engage in the effort to make it real with what we are directly facing in that moment. That confrontation is what brings a path to life.

Being mindful of our motivations and our actions, we keep ourselves from creating unnecessary suffering as best we can. And when we are not mindful, when we have broken a precept and acted in an unskillful way, we acknowledge that and wholeheartedly commit to repairing the breach and beginning again. There isn't a question of retribution or punishing ourselves. We understand the need to gather our energy to start anew instead of expending it in needless self-hatred. This is how we grow in awareness and love and how we learn to be a friend to ourselves and all of life.

There are social and political dimensions to kindness and ethics as well. There is one discourse in which the Buddha is describing a king who is about to leave his kingdom to his son. The king gave a transmission of the things he felt were most important to preserve. He told his son to be virtuous and generous. In recounting this tale, the Buddha said that as

time went on, the son, now the new king, remembered to be virtuous but he actually forgot to be generous, and because of that stealing began in the kingdom.

The king then tried to suppress this problem through instituting some severe punishments for theft. And the Buddha talked about how unsuccessful this had to be, and about how, in order to suppress the crime of stealing, the economic conditions of the people needed to be improved. That is why the king should have remembered to be generous as well as virtuous: that is what kings are for, to serve their people in those ways.

The Buddha talked about how grain and other facilities for agriculture should be provided to farmers, how capital should be given to traders, and how adequate wages should be paid to those who were employed. His advice was not to deal with the problem of stealing through punishment, but to look deeper and address the problem from that greater depth. In that way people would feel secure, and then, as he put it, they could leave their doors open. The text states that theft and violence originate in poverty, and this is what kings and governments should look at in order to pragmatically address the conditions that give rise to that kind of suffering.

The Buddha said, as many great leaders have, that people who are very hungry cannot practice morality simply as a matter of course. He spoke about how morality at least in part comes from sufficiency and about how our lives on a certain

level need to be secure for us to easily practice morality. It is much easier, for example, to steal when you are hungry, and certainly when your children are hungry. Conditions need to be created in this world so that people aren't locked into a position like that. Then kindness has a more realistic chance to flourish.

Recognizing that, we need to do the best we can to provide circumstances for everybody to be secure from lives of desperation, lest morality might seem like a nicety of the privileged. This also is an ethical imperative—our commitment to the precepts needs to be looked at in this light as well. What does stealing mean in the context of the earth's resources and the question of when we ourselves have enough? What does lying mean when related to our tendency to look the other way when someone is suffering? Can we examine all of the precepts in a social context, out of love for all beings?

What makes morality so essentially radical is seeing that we have options. We can choose a direction or a path, we can choose to let go of diversions from that path, we can choose to begin again when we've been distracted or overwhelmed. With that understanding, our day-to-day lives are like our artistic medium. Morality, the spirit of exploration, happiness, and creativity are all interwoven in how we relate to an

encounter, an opportunity, or a problem. With that spirit, the precepts are not a dry, abstract formula, but instead they are alive—in each moment of dedication they are being brought to life. Ethics are not something to just think about or to admire from a distance. They are active in this very moment, in this very thought or urge or decision, and in how we are connecting to them. This is the direct and immediate embodiment of love and understanding both for our own sake and for the benefit of all beings.

Ways to Practice Kindness through Morality

- Consider which precept is easiest for you, and see if there is a refinement that would offer you a challenge. Undertake to experiment with it for a few weeks or longer.
- Consider which precept is hardest for you. Ask yourself the question: If I loved myself enough, would this be easier for me?
- Practice material generosity. Even if what you are offering is a small amount of money or a minor possession, it is an act that opens the heart.
- Practice generosity of the spirit. Take the time to smile at someone, to wish him or her well, to offer someone a place in a line or a seat on the bus.
- Make a conscious effort to let go of self-recriminations, and move forward with new resolve if you have broken a precept.

• In the spirit of self-examination and adventure, fill in the blank for yourself in the statement, "If you want to be a rebel, _____."

six

The Intention of Kindness

Normally we have a limited sense of what we are capable of. It is usually only when we envision ourselves in extraordinary circumstances—picturing the courage we would feel if we were a mother or father protecting a child in danger, or experiencing a state of immense love filling us or great religious ardor uplifting us—that we can imagine the depth and the richness of our inner strength. But with the power of intention, we can access that strength in a wide variety of circumstances. In fact, we can have it be the bedrock of our lives.

The Buddha's own unfaltering intention was to be continually dedicated to the happiness of all beings. Soon before he died, the Buddha urged his followers to practice his teachings,

saying, "This is for the welfare of the many, for the happiness of the many, for the benefit and welfare and the happiness of beings. This is out of sympathy for the world." The Buddha had previously described his own commitment to becoming enlightened, formed so very long before those last days of his life, in just the same way: "For the welfare of the many, for the happiness of the many . . ." And he had uttered the identical phrase when he first sent out his earliest disciples to travel throughout India, urging them to teach a path to freedom. At every phase of his life, right through to the very end of it, he was committed to inclusive, wholehearted consideration of and care for others.

This kind of commitment to compassion and kindness can be made in terms of how we act, how we speak, how we focus our thoughts, and even in terms of how we respond to actions initiated by others. The Buddha was once talking to a group of monks and said to them, "You may be addressed in one of many ways as you go out on your alms rounds. People may speak to you truthfully, or they may lie to you. People may speak to you harshly, or they may speak to you very gently and softly. They may speak to you at a convenient time, or they may speak to you at an inconvenient time. They may say things you really want to hear, or they may say things you don't want to hear." He said that no matter what, the work of the monk was to respond with a heart full of lovingkindness.

From that perspective, the situation we find ourselves in doesn't govern what we care about deeply. It doesn't determine

the inner state we trust in when we feel unsteady or what we reach for to reinforce what truly matters when we feel unsure. It doesn't define who we are at our core or delineate the person we might yet be. The situation we find ourselves in isn't the source of our confidence, our courage, our tolerance, or our love. Our own heart is that source, and this heartfelt strength is expressed through *intention*.

With the force of our commitment to kindness, we develop a concentrated intention. This power of concentration allows us stability in life. Without it, every experience, circumstance, and emotion that arises can sweep us away so we feel just blown apart by life. We run after desirable things and shrink away from undesirable things that come and go in every moment. But with depth of concentration and intention, there is a feeling of centeredness, of being present, so there is emotional balance. This is not a rejection of emotion, but a sense of stability, of having a still point within, a sense of firmness and steadiness in the mind, so we can meet anything.

We need that strong power of intention to continually cut through surface appearances, to not merely settle or compromise, to not be satisfied with someone else's construct of what will make us happy. This is the Buddha's exhortation to us, his appeal to make our lives count, to live in a way that is inspired, devoted, energized, and encouraged. This is his invitation to us: to fashion our lives around what we care about deeply and to unstintingly, bravely, practice kindness—for our own sake and for the sake of all of life.

When the Buddha arose in this world 2,500 years ago, his teaching was revolutionary. In some of the philosophical systems of his time, the Sanskrit word *dharma*, which means "truth" or "true nature," had a particular connotation: the world with everything categorized according to its own intrinsic, immutable nature.

Just as it was believed that the particular nature or duty of fire was to burn, and of rocks to be hard, and of grass to grow and to be green, and of cows to eat grass and produce milk, it was believed to be the nature of some classes or castes of people to rule. For these people the use of force or violence was considered legitimate. It was believed to be the nature of certain other people to be engaged in economic production. And it was believed to be the dharma or nature of the Brahmans to read and study the scriptures and to mediate with divine forces.

There was a certain sense of destiny or fixedness to this concept. In a sense, it was viewed as a static universe, rigidly determined by birth. Everybody was seen to have a responsibility in life to grow into that given nature, to conform to that specific duty. That is what defined a good life.

Within this perspective, what was considered moral and appropriate for one type of person would be considered as

poison for another type of person. What was proper for the male Brahman—to read and study the scriptures—was considered absolutely forbidden to someone who was an outcast or a female. People who were born destined to do one thing had to fulfill that nature. For them to do something else was immoral, and there was no way for it to be made right.

The Buddha challenged this view by stating that the moral quality or potency of an action is held in the volition; it's held in the intention that is behind the action. This was very bold because his statement denied all liberating values to things that were done mindlessly, such as rituals that were performed without any presence of mind. He said that if the power of mind wasn't there, the performance itself didn't make the ceremony a sacred act.

By that teaching he also denied all ultimate value to social distinctions. It didn't matter if you were a man or a woman, wealthy or poor, a Brahman or an outcast. An act of greed performed by any of these people would have a certain kind of result. An act born out of love and kindness by any of these people would also have a certain kind of result. It didn't matter who performed it, what they looked like, where they were born, or how much prominence they had—the energy, the karma, and the living force of the action was in the intention sparking it.

Thus the entire social structure of India in those days was declared by the Buddha to be of no spiritual significance

whatsoever. He said that the only status that matters is the status of personal goodness, and this quality of personal goodness is attained through personal effort. The Buddha commented on this in many ways: "Not by birth is one a Brahman or an outcast, but by deeds." "A true Brahman is one who is gentle, who is wise and caring."

I think about what this means today, what it implies about the ways in which we classify people according to gender, race, social class, and sexual orientation, as though those classifications were all the understanding we needed, as though we could automatically determine the inner workings of people's minds and hearts once we've categorized them into their niches, as though those innermost thoughts and feelings didn't serve to distinguish one person from another and one action from another, as though the waves of hope and fear and heartache and yearning we all experience could ever be irrelevant to how someone behaves and the choices they make.

Yet we can work to not be bound by the careless assumptions we form based on meaningless classifications, and we can come to see the world in keeping with: "Not by birth is one a Brahman or an outcast, but by deeds." And we can work to view ourselves according to the same light. Do we normally put nearly as much effort into being goodhearted as we do into being seen by the world as rich or successful, or into compulsively meeting the expectations of our clan or family of origin, or into compulsively defying those very same expectations?

The Buddha's message affirms personal responsibility for our own actions, no matter who we are. All actions are born in the mind, and we cannot blame someone else for the choices we make in any situation. We cannot control which volitions will arise in our mind, but we can learn to relate to our inner world with wisdom, so that we can let go of some tendencies or nurture others, depending on what kind of person we want to be. This isn't a depressing, burdensome teaching; rather it invites us to create and, when called for, to recreate our lives committed to the force of kindness.

As we develop greater awareness, one of the things we notice is that we actually can't know the volition of an action just from seeing the action take place. For example, I might take a book and give it to someone, and it would likely look like a nice, simple thing to do. But just that motion of my hand reaching out, picking up the book, and moving it forward could be motivated by hundreds of different things.

I might think, "Well, I really like and admire this woman, and I want to perform an act of generosity. I'm going to give her the book." Or I might think, "I don't like this woman at all. It would be very inconvenient if that were known, though, so I'll just give her this book." Maybe it is, "She has a book

I really want a lot, and so if I give her this book, there is a chance she'll give me that book." Or perhaps, "Here I am on camera. If I give the woman this book, the whole world will see and I'll get a lot of praise."

These moment-to-moment intentions and the mental impulses underlying each small action are related to the larger motivations we commit to, the aspirations we uphold, the dreams we are willing to fight for. These individual intentions tie our life together. They reflect what we have dedicated our lives to, or, if we have no particular dedication, one could say they reflect the sad lack of a conscious decision to live a meaningful life. The arena of our intentions is what we look at when trying to evaluate the unity of our life and to see whether our outer world—our endeavors, pursuits, and actions—reflects our inner commitments, ideals, and values.

We need a lot of love for ourselves to want this unity, to care enough to nurture those momentary intentions that will enhance our lives, and to let go of those that will diminish it. In turning our lives in the direction of kindness, we are not operating from a sense of inner lack or incompleteness. We are not being driven by dislike of who we are right now or fear of the person we think we secretly might be deep down.

There is a word in Pali, *tejo*, which variously means heat, flame, potency, radiance, and splendor. It is this power of tejo we embody if we dedicate our lives to the force of kindness, to transforming our intentions. This is why there is such beauty in beings who are truly moral, who truly love. It has nothing to do with adherence to religious belief or tradition. This beauty comes from inner radiance, and we can see it in all kinds of people, in all kinds of different situations.

There is an unusual sort of beauty in someone like that because the foundation of this person's life is in abandoning harm and in creating well-being, and they have dedicated their lives to love. Seeing that power in others or as a vision of possibility in our mind's eye, we begin to believe that this can be true for us as well.

Insight tells us that the sense of potency and beauty and belonging and wholeness we've looked for externally—in relationships, in objects, in activity—can be found within and with all of life as we commit to kindness as the unifying principle we follow. Genuine love for ourselves takes us by the hand and has us step forward to dare many things—to seize the possibility of change, to learn to make a commitment to kindness, to patiently reinforce it, and to willingly start over again after drastically fumbling, perhaps many times, with that same commitment.

To commit to living with kindness we need to develop mindfulness as well. As we grow increasingly aware of what we are

thinking and feeling just when it is occurring, we see how that allows us to make a conscious choice to act in accord with our deeply held values. One of my favorite examples of this (or the lack thereof) is when we have been angry without quite realizing what we are feeling. In the grip of an emotion that is indistinct and indeterminate, but nonetheless gripping, we go off to the computer, write out an irate e-mail, and hastily press "send." Two hours later we may think, "Whoops. I guess I was really angry. That e-mail will only make the situation worse."

Those who use AOL as a server know that AOL has a feature where, if you send an e-mail to a recipient who is also using AOL, you are allowed to press "unsend" if the recipient has not read the message yet. Magically something will reach into his or her computer and remove that offending e-mail as though it never existed. However, most of us run back to the computer to see if the recipient has read the angry, belittling e-mail yet, and of course, inevitably it's too late. Life doesn't afford us too many opportunities to successfully press "unsend."

It is no small thing to know what we're thinking as we are thinking it, to know what we're feeling as we are feeling it. We peel away the layers of obfuscation, fear, shame, and habitual reaction to be able to say, "This is what is happening right now." The truthfulness of clear seeing is its own kind of power.

For example, sometimes we might think that we are feeling calm, but when we look more carefully, in fact what we are

feeling is timidity. We are uneasy about taking action. We are afraid to confront. We are hesitant to be forceful. From the Buddhist perspective, lack of effort is lack of courage. But this is not an easy thing to see about ourselves, so we prefer to think we are all right with things as they are. If we are developing mindfulness, we can begin to see openly what is happening and work with our thoughts and feelings more skillfully and compassionately, without denial, in order to move in the direction of wisdom and kindness.

To live in this way we also need a quality that is unpopular in our time—restraint. We tend to think of restraint as some kind of awful repression, a sort of self-mortification or torture. But what restraint really means is that we have a clarity of purpose in life, and we can devote ourselves to it. In an act of devotion to someone else, to ourselves, to a way of life, the things we are letting go of along the way are things we actually don't need.

Viewed from the outside, it might seem like, "Oh, look at that poor person; they're giving up so much." But viewed from within, relinquishing distractions and the importunities of the world, letting go of the chokehold of old habits, is like getting rid of a heavy burden. This power of restraint forms a shelter, a resting place. It gives us a place to stop, to remember our priorities, to see ourselves with love and humor and tenderness and resolve.

And we need a quality of forgiveness as well. We don't always know the right thing to do. We don't always remember

the lesson of love and humility we learned yesterday. We often get caught up in our own reactions and forget the vulnerability of the person right in front of us. We can be awfully impatient. Many times we reach out to help, to offer comfort or to have an impact, and we fall right on our faces or our intervention is met with dislike or distrust.

Maybe I hand you that book and you are feeling tired, hassled, or angry about something else and you might not express a lot of gratitude. Maybe I try to save your life, but you keep drinking like there is no tomorrow anyway. Sometimes we can't bear to see the results of our efforts spin out of our control, and we don't know if or how to keep trying to make a difference anyway. Sometimes discouragement, disillusionment, or despair heavily rule the day.

We need to be able to forgive ourselves when we stumble or forget, and based on that forgiveness to be able to reconnect to our basic intention. One of the primary tools we have in spiritual life is the understanding that everything is changing all of the time, that nothing is fixed or permanent. Because of that truth, when we make a mistake we realize that we can begin again. When we lose sight of our aspiration, we can begin again. When we stray from our chosen course, we can begin again. We need to forgive seeming failure, attempt the good right in front of us, consider the possibility of responding with love and compassion no matter what the provocation, and start over again and again and again.

We also need a quality of forgiveness toward life itself as we accept that sometimes we can only do our best and no more, and it might not seem like nearly enough. We need to accept the fact that we can't always know where our efforts of kindness will lead and that the ultimate outcome of our actions can't be seen from the limited view we have right now. We need to acknowledge with peace in our hearts how much we don't know and can't predict even as we try. We also need to know at the bottom of our hearts that we can ignite our lives with the force of kindness, and the great importance of that.

When we feel discouraged because we can't make it all better for someone the way we want to, we can come back to relying on our intention to bring some more love into this world. We can come back to remembering what we can do in the midst of what we can't do and what makes our lives meaningful. Even if we can't make someone's pain go away and we need clear boundaries in order not to be drawn into it in an unhealthy way, we can create those boundaries without also creating or upholding cynicism or indifference. We can come back to trusting the development of mindfulness, restraint, forgiveness, and love, and we can care for ourselves. That is how we can live a life suffused with kindness, not just as an ideal but in action.

Ways to Weave Kindness into Your Life through Intentions
- Start paying attention to the intentions underlying your actions. They may appear as clear thoughts in your mind,

("I'll do this, and it will give me fame and recognition") or as more amorphous urges, expectations, or yearnings.

- Remember that you cannot control which intentions and urges will arise in your mind. Our responsibility is in whether we act them out or not.

- When you have made a mistake or acted unskillfully, remember the importance of forgiving yourself so that you can gather your resolve and fully begin again.

- If you have a strong generous intention come up in your mind—one that is also reasonable (for example, not determining to give away everything)—then commit to following through with it. Even if the generous intention is at first replaced by fear ("But I may need it tomorrow," or "It's not significant enough a gift"), keep paying attention to your thoughts and feelings during and after the actual giving.

- Commit for a period of time to practice greater restraint in speech. You might consider a resolve to not speak ill of someone or to not speak about a third party. If you have something to say about someone, try to say it directly to him or her instead.

- Reflect as to whether there is an overriding dedication in your life. If so, is it manifesting in the smaller, discrete intentions impelling your actions? Resolve to bring more mindfulness to the connection between your larger goals and aspirations and your day-to-day choices.

- Practice mindfulness meditation.

MEDITATION
Experiencing the Force of Kindness

Sit comfortably, with your back erect without being strained or overarched. It is fine to sit in a chair or on an arrangement of cushions on the floor. If necessary, you can also lie down.

LISTEN TO CD TRACK 4
Mindfulness practice:
Meditating with
the force of kindness

Close your eyes and take a few deep breaths, feeling the breath as it enters your nostrils, fills your chest and abdomen, and releases. Then allow the breath to become natural, without forcing it or controlling it. Let your attention rest lightly on the feeling of the breath, like a butterfly resting on a flower, wherever you experience it most distinctly—the nostrils, the chest, or the abdomen.

Focus your attention on one breath at a time. You needn't be concerned with what has already gone by; there is no need to anticipate even the next breath. Feel the sensations of each breath—tingling, vibration, warmth, coolness, pressure, stretching, release—whatever they are and however they change. Make a quiet, mental notation of "in, out" or "rising, falling" to support your awareness of the breath.

If your mind wanders, don't be concerned. Notice whatever has captured your attention. Make a quiet mental note in acknowledgment of it, like "thinking," "anger," "joy." Let go of the thought or feeling, and return to the awareness of the breath.

If you find yourself emerging from a cloud with a lot of time having elapsed since you were last aware, that is the moment to consciously practice compassion for yourself. However long it has been or however far away your mind has wandered, you can always begin again. Practicing in this way, meditation teaches us gentleness and an ability to more easily forgive our mistakes in life and to go on.

At the end of your meditation period, go on to do a few minutes of lovingkindness practice for others in your life—your family or your community, maybe the whole planet. This forms the bridge between our inner work and our resolve to act with more kindness and love in our daily lives.

Kindness Creates Connection

The writer Wendell Berry says that "the smallest unit of health is a community." Community is another way of saying "connection." And connection is life itself. The practices of kindness inspire and deepen our connection to ourselves and to one another. They provide a path for health, for healing, for wholeness.

As we wish love, peace, and happiness for ourselves and for others, we learn to include all beings and all aspects of life, including ourselves, in our hearts. It is easy to believe that we are not capable of this, but as we untangle our conditioning, we see the immensity and abundance lying nascent within us, ready for awakening.

In doing these practices, in turning our lives toward the force of kindness, in nurturing the potential for love and compassion within, may we all find the ultimate healing truth of connection.

About the Author

SHARON SALZBERG, a student of Buddhism since 1971, has been leading meditation retreats worldwide since 1974. Influenced by her twenty-five years of study with Burmese, Indian, and Tibetan teachers, she teaches intensive awareness practice (vipassana or insight meditation) and the profound cultivation of lovingkindness and compassion (the Brahma Viharas). She is cofounder of the Barre Center for Buddhist Studies and the Insight Meditation Society, both in Massachusetts, where she lives and teaches. Sharon Salzberg is the author of several books, including *The Kindness Handbook, Faith: Trusting Your Own Deepest Experience, Lovingkindness: The Revolutionary Art of Happiness,* and *A Heart as Wide as the World*. She has also authored several Sounds True book/ audio compilations, including *Insight Meditation* (with Joseph Goldstein), *Unplug,* and *Lovingkindness Meditation.*

For more information on Sharon Salzberg and her teaching schedule, please contact:

Barre Center for Buddhist Studies
149 Lockwood Road
Barre, MA 01005
dharma.org
dharma.org/teachers/sharon/index.htm

About Sounds True

Sounds True is a multimedia publisher whose mission is to inspire and support personal transformation and spiritual awakening. Founded in 1985 and located in Boulder, Colorado, we work with many of the leading spiritual teachers, thinkers, healers, and visionary artists of our time. We strive with every title to preserve the essential "living wisdom" of the author or artist. It is our goal to create products that not only provide information to a reader or listener, but that also embody the quality of a wisdom transmission.

For those seeking genuine transformation, Sounds True is your trusted partner. At SoundsTrue.com you will find a wealth of free resources to support your journey, including exclusive weekly audio interviews, free downloads, interactive learning tools, and other special savings on all our titles.

To learn more, please visit SoundsTrue.com/bonus/free_gifts or call us toll free at 800-333-9185.

SOUNDS TRUE

P.O. Box 8010
Boulder CO 80306

Also by Sharon Salzberg
available from Sounds True

Books

The Kindness Handbook: A Practical Companion, 2008

Spoken-word Audio

Guided Meditations for Love and Wisdom:
14 Essential Practices, 2009

Insight Meditation: An In-Depth Correspondence Course, 2004

Lovingkindness Meditation: Learning to Love Through
Insight Meditation, 2004

Interactive Learning Kits

Insight Meditation (with Joseph Goldstein), 2002

Unplug: . . . For an Hour, a Day, or a Weekend, 2008

The Force of Kindness